CODING ACTIVITIES FOR
WRITING STORIES IN TWINE

Don Rauf

ROSEN PUBLISHING

Published in 2022 by The Rosen Publishing Group, Inc.
29 East 21st Street, New York, NY 10010

First Edition

Library of Congress Cataloging-in-Publication Data

Names: Rauf, Don, author.
Title: Coding activities for writing stories in Twine / Don Rauf.
Description: First edition. | New York : Rosen Publishing, 2022. |
Series: Code creator | Includes bibliographical references and index.
Identifiers: LCCN 2019017118| ISBN 9781725341111 (library bound) |
ISBN 9781725341104 (pbk.)
Subjects: LCSH: Computer games—Programming—Juvenile literature.
| Computer games—Authorship—Juvenile literature. | Twine
(Computer program)—Juvenile literature. | Plot-your-own stories—
Juvenile literature.
Classification: LCC QA76.76.C672 R388 2022 | DDC 794.8/1525—dc23
LC record available at https://lccn.loc.gov/2019017118

Manufactured in the United States of America

Some of the images in this book illustrate individuals who are models. The depictions do not imply actual situations or events.

CPSIA Compliance Information: Batch #CSRYA22. For further information contact Rosen Publishing, New York, New York at 1-800-237-9932.

Find us on

Contents

Introduction

Writing a story or article can be similar to writing computer code. In writing code, someone is putting together a series of instructions in a specific order to get a desired result. Codes are the instructions to be carried out by the computer. In writing fiction or nonfiction, someone is putting together words and sentences to take the reader on a journey to the end of a story. While words and code themselves are not creative, the way they are combined is the very essence of creativity. Writing and coding both involve an eye for detail and making sure each piece of a work supports the greater whole. Both activities involve experimenting, discovery, and improvising. Just like writing, coding can be short and to the point—or long and verbose.

Today, the worlds of coding and writing intersect with coding tools designed for storytelling. One such example is Twine, a free tool to make interactive narratives and related content. Quizzes—or pretty much anything interactive—can be easy to whip up in this format as well. Originally created by Chris Klimas in 2009, Twine is a free-to-use, open-source software suite that gives users all the tools necessary to bring together the worlds of writing and coding.

In many ways, Twine is like the books in which readers choose their own path. In these titles, the reader is placed in a narrative, and then the story moves ahead depending on what decision he or she makes. For example, the reader might be scrambling down a dark and mysterious cave and come to a fork where the tunnel splits in two. At the bottom of the page, it could say: "If you want to go down the left tunnel, turn to the next page. If you want to go down the right tunnel, turn to page 10." Readers make choices and follow the story according to their choices.

Twine works in much the same way—but in a digital format. The reader takes in the story on a computer screen and is then given some choices that will determine how the story will go. Instead of turning to a certain page, readers click on a link that will take them to a new part of the narrative. (Twine allows users to build a simple linear story, too, in which the reader just clicks ahead without making a choice—but that is not as exciting.)

For those interested in writing fiction and other types of narratives, Twine can spark new ways to think about story structure. Because Twine stories are often written from a second-person perspective (meaning they address the reader as "you"), they engage readers on a more personal level than some other forms of writing.

As a free online tool for producing interactive fiction, Twine gives writers a fresh approach to translating their stories into an interactive digital game.

Because readers must physically click to move ahead and make decisions, they are driven by curiosity to find out how a well-written Twine story will end.

The unique Twine format has inspired many people to write and code. Jane Friedhoff wrote an article for the Digital Games Research Association that argues that Twine gives power to "marginalized people" in computer science, including LGBTQ communities, racial or religious minorities, and women. It has been used as a tool for raising awareness, sharing stories, and helping others.

One of the better-known Twine creations is *Depression Quest*. This interactive fiction game was created by Zoe Tiberius Quinn to help people who are suffering from depression. *Depression Quest* is not just an interactive and interesting story—it is also a powerful educational device.

Unlike many computer games, there is typically no time pressure, frantic toggling, and rapid-fire clicking of buttons in Twine creations. Most Twine creators generally care about getting people to read and click ahead.

As a platform, Twine provides many great features. The first is that users do not need to know much about programming to figure out how to use it. It is simple and designed to be easy to learn. Even for those who may not consider themselves computer nerds, this is the perfect place to start learning about programming.

The Twine system is visually oriented. Users develop stories with a series of boxes containing text (and other content) and then connect those boxes together with arrows. Viewed from a distance, most projects look like a giant flow chart on a grid background.

To get started, go to twinery.org. As the official Twine website, it is here that the program can be downloaded or used online, no installation required. Both options have their advantages and disadvantages, and it will be possible to complete these activities using either method. One important note: using Twine in your browser will save everything, but only so long as the browser history is not deleted. Twinery.org has helpful information with a question-and-answer section, live chat, and tutorials of all kinds.

As your Twine story comes together, it will be necessary to incorporate HTML (Hypertext Markup Language) and CSS (Cascading Style Sheets), which are considered the languages of the internet. Another popular language in this field is JavaScript, but it is a little more complex. That said, it is also powerful and useful for doing cool things within a Twine project.

Luckily, because HTML and CSS are so widespread,

Unlike most video games, in which precision, accuracy, and reflexes are the most important tools for success, Twine games are generally more relaxed.

there are plenty of resources for learning more about the coding that goes into making interactive Twine stories. Because many coding enthusiasts love sharing their work, it is often possible to search online and find just the right chunk of code needed to perform different functions—maybe including an image or letting the reader tally up points for certain answers.

After completing a Twine project, it can be saved as a URL address or HTML file and shared with friends and family. However, while others will be able to read the

Twine is a great introduction to coding with more versatile languages, like hypertext markup language (HTML), Cascading Style Sheets (CSS), and JavaScript.

story on a computer, it is necessary to find a site that will host all the interactive content so others can see it. Philome.la (http://www.philome.la) offers free hosting for Twine tales and games; Twinery.org offers links to other free hosting sites as well.

Aside from Twine, there are other software tools available for creating interactive fiction, most allowing for the integration of graphics and multimedia elements. These include the Elm Narrative Engine, Ren'Py, Quest, Squiffy, and TADS (Text Adventure Development System). They are all worth exploring after Twine.

Activity 1

Learning Twine Basics: All About Passages and Links

In Twine, passages are blocks of text and links are the paths that move between these passages. Think of links like a computerized way of turning a page. The squares of text, called passages, lay out on a neat map or grid and then the creator links them together by using simple code, which can be identified by looking for text set inside square brackets.

After starting up Twine, there should be a page with a few options in a side panel. Start off by clicking on the +Story button to begin; a prompt will appear and ask for a story name—go with "Missing Fido." The first thing that shows up in a new Twine story is a passage box on the story map. This is where everything in the story takes place. Double-clicking on the passage box brings up three new boxes: the name ("Untitled Passage" for now), the tag (nothing for now) and the text box (which currently says "Double-click this passage to edit it"). The title and text boxes have obvious uses, and the tags will be covered later.

A lot of first Twine passages are titled "Start" because this will instantly show where this particular story begins. The coder is the only person who will see this; titles are mainly used to label items and help organize, but no one reading the Twine story later on will see it.

Try writing a short scene to establish a story in this first passage's text box. Here is an example of a brief scene:

Your dog has run out of the house. You dash out the front door searching for her.

Pretty basic, but it sets the stage for the story. To take the reader to the next step, it is time to bring links into play. Links are created by putting a sentence within two square brackets. Twine is designed to give the reader options, so try to link to two possible actions after the opening scene. For example:

[[You turn to the right and go to a neighbor pushing a baby carriage.]]

[[You go to the left, toward the park.]]

Close out of the opening passage and look at the story map. By adding two links in the original passage, Twine automatically created two new passages—one for each link—that are connected to the start by single-direction arrows. Hit the Play button at the bottom of the screen to see the results on linking. Pressing Play opens up the story, where the opening text and the two passages will be visible—but it will not show the coding brackets surrounding the linking text. Click on one of these sentences and the story proceeds to the next passage. For now, there is nothing else in the story, so return to the main story map.

Now, try adding links to each of the two previous passages. Remember: links will always go inside a passage's text box. Here is an example. In the passage named "You turn to the right and go to a neighbor pushing a baby carriage":

[[You ask her if she's seen Fido.]]

[[Her dog tries to bite you and you run the opposite direction.]]

In the passage "You go to the left, toward the park":

In the park, you see a large man with balloons.

[[You ask him if he's seen your dog.]]

[[You run directly to the park.]]

With these links, there are four new passages in place. The boxes of text on the story map may get crowded or overlap at this point, but they can be dragged and placed in any position without harming the code.

Press the Play button to test out the interactive story. Though this story does not go anywhere—yet—it has been set up with the important basic features of Twine with its links and passages.

Activity 2

Passages and Links: Part Two

To keep things organized, it will sometimes be necessary to give a linked passage a title that is different from the linked text. Though this may sound complex, it is actually pretty simple. Check out this example. In the passage named "You ask her if she's seen Fido," add in the following:

"She silently points inside her baby [[carriage|There's Fido]]."

By using the straight vertical line—called a pipe—the story is coded to show the reader a link that is activated when the reader clicks the word "carriage," but on the map, that linked passage will be titled "There's Fido." This helps the writer identify an element of the story, but the reader will not have to see it. Inserting the pipe is easy: just press the shift key and the backslash key.

It is also possible to link two or more passages to the same passage, as in this example. Go to the passage box titled "You ask him if he's seen your dog" and add:

"The balloon man silently points inside [[a box by his feet|There's Fido]]."

By putting in "There's Fido" after the pipe, this passage will now be connected to the same "There's Fido" passage.

In the "There's Fido" passage, type in:

"There's Fido. He is looking guilty and has your favorite hat in his mouth. THE END."

Now there are two passages that link to the end of the story.

To review a story from a new starting point, just single-click on the passage in which it should start and click on the icon for more options. This will feature a Start Story Here button; click that and play the story—it will now begin from that point. The starting passage of a story in Twine is symbolized by the green rocket ship icon.

Creating links is easy, and deleting them is similarly simple. If a linked passage is erased, a red X symbol will appear on the map. This can be fixed by going back to the passage and writing in a new link to replace the one that was trashed. Then the red X will disappear and there will instead be a link to the new information that should be displayed.

If something is not working as expected, click the arrow next to the story title on the lower left of the map to reveal a list of options. Select View Proofing Copy from this menu. This generates an easy-to-read text document to review all the instructions and passages that have been written for the story.

Check for broken links by looking for anything tinted in red on the story map. Clicking on Story Statistics in the title menu will bring up the number of characters, words, passages, links, and broken links. If there are zero broken links, everything should be in good shape.

Styling Your Story: Simple Text Formatting

The text that comes default with Twine is fine, but sometimes it is fun—or useful—to add advanced style and creativity options. With some simple coding, it is easy to adjust text in a number of ways. For adding text styles in Twine, the common format is to use a language called Harlowe. To bold a word, put it between two asterisks or quote marks, as in **Bold** or "Bold." To italicize, use single asterisks or two slashes, as in *Italics* or //Italics//.

To return to the previous example story about Fido, change the text in the Start passage to read: "Your **dog** has *run* out of the house. You dash out the front door searching for her." Check out what these adjustments do to the text by playing the story.

To make words both bold and italic, simply include three asterisks on either side, as in ***bold and italics***. Adding an underline is done by formatting as <u>underlined</u>. Two other Harlowe text formatting codes that might useful are ^^superscript^^ and ~~strikethrough~~.

To make a bulleted list, use asterisks in the code, which then appear as the asterisks in the list. Here is an example:

*yes

*no

*maybe

There are many tricks available to make the text operate in different ways. Try this one out: write the line "Your dog has disappeared" and have the whole sentence disappear when the reader scrolls over it. How is this possible? This involves using HTML code within Twine.

In a Twine passage box, type:

```
<div class="disappeared">Your dog has disappeared. See what happens when you scroll over this sentence. </div>
```

This is an HTML code that is instructing the computer to apply a certain attribute to specific text. It is defining a division (div) or section, and the class portion means that the code is going to give that line of text a certain attribute—in this case, the attribute will be that the text disappears when it is scrolled over.

The key here is to now type some code into a style sheet so it will instruct the story to behave this way. To do so, open up the story options menu on the map and select Edit Story Stylesheet. This will allow you to make changes to the overall style of the story. It is the same as the CSS (Cascading Style Sheet) coding that is used in website design. In the stylesheet, type:

```
.disappeared:hover {
opacity: 0;
transition: 1s all ease;
}
```

When an instruction is introduced with a dot or period, as it is here, it is telling the computer to apply code to the specified element (in this case, "disappeared"). Opacity tells the text to disappear; "1s all ease" is used to apply a fade-out effect. Now, click Play and mouse over the text in this passage—it should fade out and reappear only when the cursor is moved.

The default language for Twine—which can be used for basic text effects—is Harlowe. Harlowe itself is written in the computer language JavaScript, and coding in this format reduces the amount of code that would otherwise be necessary for Twine to operate.

Twine also allows for other formats and languages, however, depending on user preference. Click on the story options menu and there is an option to Change Story Format. Here, there are different versions of Harlowe and other formats, named Snowman and SugarCube.

Some prefer using SugarCube because it can be easier to handle media, links, and graphic user interface elements, such as check boxes, buttons, sliders, droplists, and text boxes. Because the code is laid out in a way that may be easier to follow, some of the following activities will use SugarCube.

Getting Fancy: Updating Your Look

Modifying or adding a text effect is all well and good, but what about changing an actual font? It is possible to change fonts and sizes in Twine, but it is a little more complicated. Again, it will involve editing the story stylesheet, which is accessed by selecting Edit Story Stylesheet in the story menu.

To explain what this stylesheet does more directly: when CSS code is typed here, it is altering the standard built-in code that Twine uses. The basic construction for playing around with fonts is as follows:

```
body, tw-story
{
    font-family: Futura;
    font-size: 40px;
}
```

This code will change all the story's text to the Futura font and make it bigger. There are many font styles to choose from. Futura is a pretty common font, so most people should be able to display the text on their computer if they run this story in Twine. However, if someone tries to insert a special or rare font, users may not be able to see any text at all when they run the game. For this reason, it is important to stick with fonts that are likely to work for a wide range of people.

The other component in this code is the size element: the 40px (pixels), which is the same as 30pt (point). Pixels are small units that are used to display images on any computer screen. One pixel is one tiny visual square on the screen. A typical high-definition computer monitor or television will have 2,073,600 pixels—1,920 pixels across and 1,080 pixels down. It is also possible to use percentages to increase or lower the font size in Twine; for example, font-size: 20% or font-size 120%.

Points, contrasted with pixels, are fixed units of type size, traditionally used in print. Font size can be set using points, but for onscreen Twine design, pixel measures are more accurate.

In addition to size and shape, Twine allows users to change font colors. Here is a sample that makes passages yellow and links red:

```
tw-passage
{
  color: yellow;
}
tw-link
{
  color: red;
}
```

The background color can also be manipulated in a similar way:

```
tw-passage

{

  background-color: green;

}
```

That is all well and good, but what about setting certain words in one color and certain words in another size? To make particular changes like that, the code is inserted directly into a passage box. For example, if you wanted the word "dog" to suddenly be big and blue, you could type ""Dog"" into a passage. This instructs the story to make the word "Dog" take on the specific appearance in one particular place.

It is also possible to change the entire background of the story's screen. The default color is black, but if you wanted to change it to white, for example, this code would need to be added to the stylesheet:

```
tw-story {

background-color: white;

}
```

For more advanced color design, Twine also supports using different shades—inserting these complex colors requires using a code called a hex triplet. To see choices, visit the website for Adobe Color (https://color.adobe.com) or Paletton (http://paletton.com).

For a more interesting background, try inserting an image using a .jpeg file that is already online. Using this code, the Twine story grabs the image and displays it for anyone reading the story to see. The generic code is "background-image: url(https://nameoffile.jpg)."

Here is an example that will change the background to display an ocean image:

```
}


tw-story {


background-image:  url(https://upload.wikimedia.org/
   wikipedia/commons/e/e0/Clouds_over_the_Atlantic_
   Ocean.jpg)


}
```

Note that Twine will only display this image if the previous background color code from above is removed from the stylesheet. With this code, an ocean view will be present throughout the entire Twine tale.

Activity 5

A Visual Bang: Inserting an Image into Your Story

Sometimes, adding a fun image or two will help out a story. It is possible to link to a .jpg digital image that already exists online using HTML. Keep in mind that if there is a mistake in the coding and something is not functioning right, Twine will often display an error message right away telling you that something has been done wrong. Of course, it will also be obvious that something is wrong if the image does not appear once the Twine game is tested.

Since this example story is about a dog, try inserting an image of a dog to start out the story. This visual will help hook readers into the story right away. In the starting passage, insert the following:

Your **dog** has *run* out of the house. You dash out the front door searching for her.

<img src="https://upload.wikimedia.org/wikipedia/commons/5/50/GoldenRetriver_agility_tunnel_wb.jpg" width="600" height="300">

This should link you to an image of a dog that is hosted on Wikipedia. There are a variety of images like this—in .jpg formats—all over the internet, so feel free to search out and select any image that goes along with whatever story or project you are working on. It is important to remember, however, that the URL must end in ".jpg." After searching out a picture and ensuring that it ends with ".jpg," all it takes to import that image into Twine is highlighting the exact URL for the image and cutting and pasting it into the appropriate passage box.

By tagging the information "img," the computer and browser know it should be looking out for HTML code about an image. The "src" portion signals the exact URL source to which the software should be trying to connect.

In this example as well, the dimensions are being adjusted to make the image fit and look nice on the screen. The "alt="GoldenRetriver_agility_tunnel_wb.jpg" is used to identify the image, and that segment of the code is followed by the measures of width and height. As before, these numbers represent the width and height in pixels, and they can be adjusted to meet nearly any specifications or preferences. Play around with these numbers and see how it will change the appearance of the dog image. Some sizes will certainly look better than others, and it is up to the creator to make Twine images look good.

The location of the image can also be changed. If the image should align on the right side of the screen, for example, the style needs to be coded differently—like so:

```
<img src="https://upload.wikimedia.org/wikipedia/
   commons/5/50/GoldenRetriver_agility_tunnel_
   wb.jpg" style="float: right"; width="600"
   height="300">
```

The only thing that needs to be added is the section that changes the style—"style="float: right""—which, in this case, tells the image to appear on the right of the screen.

There are many ways to display images, and most of the code required to modify images is easily available by searching online.

Twine also supports .gif file formats. A GIF image is a short, continually looping animation without any sound. Try plugging in this GIF of a dog in the starting passage—again using HTML code:

```
<img src=https://media.giphy.com/media
  /YIW0KqAQShjCE/giphy.gif>
```

Videos can offer even more. There are a lot of ways to link up a video to Twine, but an easy first step is to start with a YouTube video. Find a video that fits whatever the project requires and look for a button labeled Share. Clicking this button on a YouTube video will open another window with some options. Clicking Embed will open another new window, this time displaying the exact HTML code necessary for sharing the video in a Twine story. It should look something like this:

```
<iframe width="560" height="315" src="[URL will
  be here]" frameborder="0" allow="accelerometer;
  autoplay; encrypted-media; gyroscope; picture-in-
  picture" allowfullscreen></iframe>
```

All it takes to import this video into a Twine story is copying and pasting that HTML code chunk into whichever passage should feature the video. Then, when people play through the game, they will be presented with a window that plays the video.

Activity 6

Change Is Good: Using Variables

Variables are important parts of any software suite or programming language. Simply put, a variable is an element that the program or user can change. If a Twine story sets up a variable in its code, the reader can input her or his own information that will appear in a story or be used to perform other calculations behind the scenes. Here is a simple example to get started.

First, make a new story titled "Dracula's House Adventure." On the opening story map, open up the story menu and select the option to Change Story Format. In the new window that appears, select the latest version of SugarCube. This will allow the story to use coding elements from the SugarCube language, which will help with the creation of variables.

With all that settled, copy the following text into the starting passage, which should be renamed "Welcome to Dracula's House":

Thank you for coming to Dracula's House.

To come inside, you must enter your name:

<<textbox "$name" "">>

When you're done, click [[here|Welcome]] to come in.

Note that <<textbox>> creates a box in which the reader can write his or her name. The box is called

"$name" because a $ symbol in Twine identifies an element as a variable. People can insert whatever name they like in the box.

Going back to your map, the starting passage will be to the new "Welcome" passage. In this box, type:

Welcome, $name, to the House of Dracula!

Though it looks a little funny on the back end, the "$name" here will call back to whatever name the user entered on the first screen. Using this variable technique, people reading the story can include their own name, which makes things more exciting.

Click the Play button to test things out so far, and an empty box will appear on the first screen—it is here that users will enter their names. Then, when they click to move forward, they will see their name in the next screen.

Variables are useful for more than just entering and keeping track of a name. They can also be used to set up conditional passages. In the "Welcome" passage, beneath the text that is already there, type:

Would you like to visit the bathroom or the kitchen first?

Type which room you would like to see first:

<<textbox "$room" "">>

Click [[here|Next room]] to move forward.

This passage now presents readers with two choices: do they move to the kitchen or to the bathroom? To handle their input, it will be necessary to make a branch in the newly created "Next room" passage. Copy this into that new passage box:

```
<<if $room is "bathroom">>This is Dracula's toilet!
  Sorry, there are no mirrors!
<</if>>
<<if $room is "kitchen">>This is Dracula's kitchen. That
  is not ketchup in that bottle!
<</if>>
```

Now, depending on which word readers entered, they will be taken to the appropriate room. However, what if someone writes in a variable that does not exist—like "garage"? Nothing will happen, and that is not good. Instead of leaving readers hanging, insert some code in the "Next room" passage that will tell readers that they got it wrong:

```
You've done something wrong. Click [[here]] to
  try again.
```

This text will pop up if readers do not put in "bathroom" or "kitchen." The [[here]] will take them back to the previous passage. Wait, though—if the code is set up like this, readers will be shown the failure message even if they enter a valid word. A better way to set up the conditional options in the "Next room" passage is like this:

```
<<if $room is "bathroom">>This is Dracula's toilet!
  Sorry, there are no mirrors!
```

```
<<elseif $room is "kitchen">>This is Dracula's kitchen.
  That is not ketchup in that bottle!
<<else>> You've done something wrong. Click [[here]]
  to try again.
<</if>>
```

The <<elseif>> segment here tells the computer to show the reader other information if the reader types in "kitchen" instead of "bathroom." Then, the <<else>> will instead make the screen say that something has gone wrong if readers have not typed either of the two choices, and it gives them the opportunity to click back and try again.

Boolean Action: Using a True or False Setup

One of the best things about a Twine story is that reader input can have an impact on the end result. Variables can keep track of player options and choices across a story, and Twine can look at those variables when it comes time to end the story—and even provide a different ending that depends on the choices readers make. The example in this activity will use a true or false setup, often called a Boolean variable or just a Boolean. An old and important concept in programming, a Boolean is simply data that can have only one of two values: typically true or false. The conditional statements explained earlier are some examples of a Boolean variable. The basic application of true-or-false coding in Twine is as follows: if the situation is true and meets a condition, the reader advances in the story; if the reader chooses a different path, the situation is false, and she or he ends the story in a completely different, unsuccessful way.

To continue "Dracula's House Adventure," perhaps the reader must befriend an owl to advance the plot. In the "Next room" passage, copy the following:

```
<<if $room is "bathroom">>This is Dracula's toilet!
Sorry, there are no mirrors! You continue to the
[[dining room]].
```

```
<<elseif $room is "kitchen">>This is Dracula's kitchen.
That is not ketchup in that bottle! You pick up some
garlic and continue to the [[next room|Front door]].
```

```
<<else>> You've done something wrong. Click [[here]]
to try again.
```

```
<</if>>
```

This updated code will create some new links, and each new passage will require some code. In the "dining room" passage, type this:

```
<<set $hasowl to true>>
```

You are in a large old spooky dining room. Dracula is sitting at the head of the table. He says, "I'm so glad I can have you for dinner!" You run in horror out the front door and into the woods.

As you stand frightened in the woods, an owl flies up and lands on your shoulder. Much to your surprise, he can talk!

"Dracula loves owls," he says. "Let's go back to the house; I have an idea on how to scare him off."

You go with the owl back to the front door and ring the [[bell]].

The "Front door" passage needs some options now, as well:

Igor, Dracula's servant, finds you in the entryway.

"Sorry," he says. "Here's the front door. I'm afraid you'll have to leave. Garlic gives the Count an upset stomach."

You walk off into the woods, but after a few steps, you decide that you must get back in Dracula's house and defeat him.

You return to the front door of Dracula's house and ring the [[bell]].
<<set $hasowl to false>>

Note that the variable <<set $hasowl to true>> advances the action, while <<set $hasowl to false>> will bring the action to a close. However, both paths of action link to the passage called "bell." This passage will be the last stop for anyone who did not meet the owl:

After waiting a moment, Igor, the servant, answers the door.

"Back so soon, $name?," he says.

```
<<if $hasowl is true>> When Igor sees the owl, his eyes
    widen and he says, "Please come in, $name."
You walk back into the [[house]].
<<else>> Igor looks you up and down. "Why didn't you
    bring an owl, $name? Sorry, you can't come back in.
    Please throw this bag of trash away in the bin at the
    end of the driveway on your way home. Bye, $name."
THE END
<</if>>
```

The Boolean check here determines, as the code implies, whether readers made the right choice and made a feathered friend. If they did not, their story is over—but if they did, they get to experience the "house" passage:

You step into the house and see Dracula. He looks at you, smiling, and says, "I'm so happy you brought me an owl!"

The owl gives you a quick wink, then suddenly yells, "BOO!"

Dracula is so shocked he jumps from the nearest window and runs away—never to be seen again.

THE END

By adding in the code <<if $hasowl is true>> and <<else>>, Boolean variables are having a real, noticeable effect on the story.

Activity 8

Get Smart: Making a Quiz

Twine is a versatile tool. In addition to being the perfect software for interactive fiction, it can also be used for setting up a quiz. Here are some ideas on how to get one going.

Begin a new story and title it "Super Quiz." The opening passage should be named "Start." Inside that passage, insert the following:

"Super Quiz"

Question 1

The Swedish flag is blue and __.

[[a. yellow]]

[[b. red]]

[[c. green]]

[[d. purple]]

Remember that surrounding text by two single quotes will make it bold. That is kind of exciting, but a quiz should have a little more pizzazz. Replace the plain "Super Quiz" text with this code:

"Super Quiz"

This tells the computer that the Super Quiz text should be red, 150 percent the size, and set in bold.

Each answer—in this case, the four color options—will link to a separate passage; three will be incorrect, and one will be correct. In the "a. yellow" passage, the quiz taker should be congratulated:

That's right! You can move on to [[Question 2]].

In the three other passage boxes, however, quiz takers will have to try again and move back to the first question:

Sorry! That's not right. [[Try again|Start]].

In the new "Question 2" passage, there needs to be, well, another question:

Question 2
What is the fastest land animal in the world?

[[a. the antelope]]
[[b. the lion]]
[[c. the cheetah]]
[[d. the rabbit]]

The correct passage will be "c. the cheetah," so copy this:

That's right! The cheetah can run up to 60 miles per hour! You can move on to [[Question 3]].

The other, incorrect passages should redirect readers back so they can try again:

Sorry! That's not right. [[Try again|Question 2]].

A quiz in Twine is not limited to multiple-choice questions. To mix things up, why not add a fill-in-the-blank question? The "Question 3" passage does just that:

Question 3

Who was the first president of the United States?

<<textbox "$answer" "">>

Click [[here|Filled answer]] to move on.

This will give quiz takers a text box so they can write their own answer. Evaluating the user input is a little tricky, however. In the "Filled answer" passage, type:

<<if $answer is "George Washington">>That's right! You can move on to [[Question 4]].

<<elseif $answer is "Washington">>Almost, but we need his first name, too. Click [[here|Question 3]] to try again.

<<else>> Sorry! That's not right. Click [[here|Question 3]] to try again.

<</if>>

This gives Twine three options for evaluating an answer: it is either fully correct, partially correct, or totally wrong. The instructions displayed by the program will move readers along if they have the right answer, but send the reader back if not.

To change the look and feel of the quiz, it could be fun to use buttons, which are called radiobuttons in Twine. Try out some buttons in "Question 4":

Question 4

What is the most popular fruit in America?

* <<radiobutton "$fruit" "Apples" checked>> Apples

* <<radiobutton "$fruit" "Bananas">> Bananas

* <<radiobutton "$fruit" "Blueberries">> Blueberries

* <<radiobutton "$fruit" "Grapes">> Grapes

Click [[here|Question 4 Possibles]] to move on

This codes the quiz to show a clickable button for each possible answer, and the variable for $fruit sets up the "Question 4 Possibles" passage to evaluate the answer in an if-else format:

<<if $fruit is "Bananas">>That's right! You can move on. <<button "[[CLICK HERE|Question 5]]">><</button>>

<<else>>Sorry! That's not right. Click [[here|Question 4]] to try again

<</if>>

This mixes things up visually again, giving readers a button with the words "CLICK HERE" inside if they got it right. The reader can click this and then move to Question 5.

Alternatively, try setting up the "Question 4" passage like this:

Question 4

What is the most popular fruit in America?

<<button "[[Apples|Wrong]]">><</button>>

<<button "[[Bananas|Right]]">><</button>>

<<button "[[Blueberries|Wrong]]">><</button>>

<<button "[[Grapes|Wrong]]">><</button>>

Then, in the "Wrong" passage, type:

Sorry! That's not right. Click [[here|Question 4]] to try again.

In the "Right" passage, write:

That's right! Here's [[the last question|Question 5]].

Activity 9

Know the Score: Setting Up a Point System

Creating a quiz that allows users to freely go back and change their answers is easy to make, but it is not really how quizzes are supposed to work. Instead, points should be awarded for a correct answer, and points should be deducted for an incorrect answer. Luckily, Twine provides the coding tools to set up a point system.

A scoring system will be a changing variable, so it will be necessary to use the $ symbol to indicate the element that is changing in the quiz. In the "Start" passage of the "Super Quiz" story, add in the following:

<<set $score to 0>>

When something is "set" at the Start, the variable is being established for use throughout the rest of the quiz (or story or whatever is being worked on). In the quiz as it is right now, the correct answer for the first question is yellow. So, in the "a. yellow," passage add in:

Score: <<print $score + 1>>

The "print" in this short bit of code is telling the computer to display whatever follows the word "print." The "$score + 1" component is called an expression. An expression is the result of a mathematical formula. In this case, the reader got the question right, so the score should display ("print") as 1, which is the result of the mathematical formula: $score + 1.

This is all well and good, but the reader's score needs to go up by one point for every question answered correctly. So, the passage titled "c. cheetah" (the correct answer for the second question), type:

Score: <<print $score + 2>>

The variable score changes as it goes along with each right answer. The reader should now see a "Score: 2" on the screen. The "Question 3" passage was set up a little differently, but the idea is the same for the "Filled answer" passage. Simply change the first line to:

<<if $answer is "George Washington">>That's right! You can move on to [[Question 4]]. <<print $score + 3>>

For the final answer's "Right" passage, copy this:

That's right! Score: <<print $score + 4>>

Congratulations, you have a perfect score of 4!

Though this method was good for adding up points, it did not do anything to take away points when someone gets an answer wrong. Try setting up a system that does not allow quiz takers to get endless chances to correct their answers. To do this, the $score variable in the "Start" passage will stay the same. However, the "a. yellow" passage will need to change:

That's right! You can move on to [[Question 2]].

Score: <<print $score += 1>>.

The passages for the wrong answers will need to change as well:

Sorry! That's not right. You lose a point.

Score: <<print $score -1>>

Try [[Question 2][$score -= 1]].

Repeat this process for the next question's right and wrong passages as well. In "c. cheetah":

That's right! The cheetah can run up to 60 miles per hour! You can move on to [[Question 3]].

Score: <<print $score += 1>>

The three incorrect answer passages should look like this:

Sorry. That's not right. You lose a point.

Score: <<print $score -1>>.

Try [[Question 3][$score -= 1]].

Once again, things get a little more complex for the third question. In the "Filled answer" passage, copy the following:

<<if $answer is "George Washington">>That's right! You can move on to [[Question 4]]. Score: <<print $score += 1>>

<<elseif $answer is "Washington">>Almost, but we need his first name, too. Click [[here|Question 3]] to try again.

<<else>> Sorry!

That's not right.

Score: <<print $score -1>>.

Click [[here|Question 4][$score -= 1]] to move on

<</if>>

Finally, change up the "Question 4" passage so it looks like this:

Question 4

What is the most popular fruit in America?

<<button "[[Apples|Wrong][$score -= 1]]">><</button>>

<<button "[[Bananas|Right][$score += 1]]">><</button>>

<<button "[[Blueberries|Wrong][$score -= 1]]">><</button>>

<<button "[[Grapes|Wrong][$score -= 1]]">><</button>>

This will set up the "Super Quiz" to subtract a point for any wrong final answer and add a point for a correct final answer. In the "Wrong" passage, write:

Wrong. Sorry!

Your grand total score is <<print $score>>.

```
<<if $score == 3>>That's pretty good. You might want
   to try one more time for a perfect score.
<<elseif $score == 2>>That's ho-hum. I think you can do
   better than that!
<<elseif $score == 1>> That's pretty bad! You better try
   again!
<<else>> That's awful. You better try again!
</if>>
```
Click [[here|Start]] if you'd like to try again.

The last step in this whole process is to change the "Right" passage:

That's right!

Your grand total score is <<print $score>>.

```
<<if $score == 4>>Fantastic! You are a genius!
<<elseif $score == 3>>That's pretty good. You might
   want to try one more time for a perfect score.
<<elseif $score == 2>>That's ho-hum. I think you can do
   better than that!
<<elseif $score == 1>> That's pretty bad! You better try
   again!
<<else>> That's awful. You better try again!
</if>>
```
Click [[here|Start]] if you'd like to try again.

That is the miniature "Super Quiz" from start to finish. Of course, it is easy to expand or modify everything in Twine, so feel free to change the questions or answers to something more interesting. Additionally, it is still possible to add images, colors, text effects, and more to a quiz, so customize until the cows come home.

Activity 10

Get Organized: Managing Your Content

In addition to the coding components that are behind a fun Twine experience, there is a lot of housekeeping. Ideally, the images in a Twine project should be managed and stored in a place that the creator can control directly. Organizing everything, however, goes beyond just making a simple HTML file of the story. It is necessary to create a file that stores both the HTML file and the media assets (images, videos, music, etc.) that are associated with a particular Twine project.

Return to the "Missing Fido" story to experiment with getting organized. Create a new folder on your desktop—name it "Missing Fido." Then, open the story menu at the bottom left of the screen and select Publish to File. Doing so will generate an HTML file of the game. Open this up, then highlight the URL and slide it into the "Missing Fido" folder. It should look something like this: file:///Users/username/Downloads/Missing%20 Fido%202.html

Within the "Missing Fido" folder, create two new folders: "Images" and "Music."

Take a personal photo of a dog or draw a picture of a dog—it does not matter which, but do not use a picture from the internet. Import the dog image to your computer and save it as "Dog.jpg." This image can then be inserted into the Twine story by using something called a relative path. Use the following code to make this relative path:

```
<img src="Images/Dog.jpg" />
```

When the story is published now, the image should appear.

The same thing can be done with music files, typically saved as MP3 files. It is important to note that if the Twine project is being used publicly, it may not use any music that is copyrighted by someone else. However, for private use and experimentation, it is acceptable to use MP3 files on your computer. The internet is also a powerful resource for finding copyright-free music.

After locating a tune that will work for a Twine project—for example, a file called "DogSong.mp3"—place it into the project's "Music" folder. Then, in the story itself, it is necessary to create a unique passage named "StoryInit" that is not linked to anything. This will allow you to import and incorporate the music file.

Format the story so it uses the most updated version of SugarCube. To load the MP3, Twine requires a bit of code called a macro (a single instruction that expands automatically into a set of instructions to perform a particular task). In Twine, macro is a predefined piece of code that can be inserted into a passage. The macro to store audio is <<cahcheaudio>>; in this example:

```
<<cacheaudio "DogSong" "music/DogSong.mp3">>
```

By putting DogSong in quotes, the file is given that identifying title. To get this to play when the story starts, a command needs to be issued in the "Start" passage:

<<audio DogSong play>>

As with an image, it is necessary to publish the story before the audio will play. It is also possible to change up the music by putting additional songs into the project's "Music" folder. Maybe a specific song— "BarkSong.mp3," for example—should play in only one passage. After adding that MP3 file to the "Music" folder, go back to your StoryInit passage and add in the code:

<<cacheaudio "BarkSong" "music/BarkSong.mp3">>

Then, select the passage in which the DogSong should stop playing and BarkSong should start up. Write a macro as follows, and it will be music to the reader's ears:

<<audio DogSong stop>>

<<audio BarkSong play>>

Career Connections

For those who are uncertain if coding and programming are the right choice for them, Twine offers an entertaining way to test the waters. The format allows users to build an interactive story with some very basic coding know-how. As software becomes more and more familiar, it features enough options to meet a coder's advanced needs or help teach more complex types of programming.

Although it is difficult to find anyone making a career out of Twine design alone, some people have had success selling their Twine-based stories and games on popular PC gaming platforms, such as Steam.

Writers take note: Twine makes you think in a way that really propels the action along. To explore the endless possibilities of creativity in Twine, check out the Interactive Fiction Database (IFDB) at https://ifdb.tads.org. By using these games as inspiration, you can hone your skills as a writer and open your work up to new audiences.

In this computer-driven world, developing some coding talent—such as learning HTML in Twine—can pay off big-time. Though job opportunities for computer programmers, specifically, are expected to slightly decline between 2016 and 2026, according to the Bureau of Labor Statistics (BLS), occupations that require computer knowledge overall will increase by 13 percent. Those who excel in the field of computer

Getting a grasp on how coding works can help in almost any career. Learning more about computer programming can open doors to rewarding—and well-paid—opportunities.

science often find it very rewarding, both creatively and financially. The BLS reported that computer programmers earned an average of $86,320 in May 2018.

Those who thrive in the computer industry typically enjoy problem solving and logic puzzles. The work can require great patience—sometimes, lines of code will not produce the desired results, and coders have to try out many solutions before finding the answer. The process of finding programming mistakes and fixing them is called debugging. Coders must catalog their efforts, developing libraries of code to make future coding easier. (Incidentally, it is possible to find tons of coding libraries online for free.)

Once a person gets comfortable coding and programming, he or she may want to advance to an occupation as a software developer. While coders come up with the lines of instructions to make programs function, developers create and conceive the overall software. They typically have the big picture in mind, coming up with a product (such as a game) to fulfill an important need. Software developers come up with browsers, such as Firefox and Safari, and they are behind popular tools, such as Adobe's Photoshop and Microsoft Word. They think of the concept and outline how the software can be created, then pass some of the actual code writing to the programmers.

Twine can open doors into the gaming world; in fact, the most common use of the platform is to build computer games. Often, games require players to make choices that will influence if they win or lose. Pick up the dagger and fight off the monster, for example, or maybe a character opens a hatch and escapes to the roof. These types of scenes unfold repeatedly in the gaming world. Coders create the environment, characters, look, and feel of a game, most commonly turning to slick, cutting-edge graphics. Twine games have similar themes, but they are often conveyed using words, rather than actual visual elements.

While Twine can lay a foundation for learning programming, those who want to pursue an advanced career involving computers need to learn more languages. Many 3D games are written in the languages

C or C++, for example. Java is considered a versatile language, and it is often used for games that are playable on mobile devices. Here some of the top programming languages to consider mastering beyond the basics taught in Twine:

- **C:** Known as a general-purpose language, C dates back to 1972. The language is used for a wide variety of platforms and computer operating systems.
- **C++:** This variant of C works on a range of platforms, such as Windows, macOS, and UNIX. For years, C++ has remained a very popular programming language worldwide.
- **C#:** This language is a variation of C and C++ and is commonly used in the Unity® game engine.
- **Java:** Java routinely ranks among the top popular languages; despite their names, Java and JavaScript are completely different.
- **Python:** Widely used for diverse tasks—ranging from web development to game design to analyzing data—Python is hugely popular. Parts of Google are written in Python, as are some blockbuster games.
- **Ruby:** This is a dynamic, open-source programming language with a focus on simplicity and productivity. Hulu and Twitter are two of the major companies that use Ruby for their programming.

Though the path of learning computer programming is far from easy, there are dozens of free and paid-for online resources and tutorials for learning all these common languages and more.

Before moving on to complex and diverse languages, it may be helpful to turn toward a simple programming

platform, such as Scratch. Primarily designed to show young people how to animate and make games, Scratch is a powerful educational tool. Also check out Alice, a block-based programming environment that makes it easy to create animations, build interactive narratives, or program simple games. Like Twine, these basic platforms offer beginners a way to break into more advanced forms of coding.

Anyone serious about mastering programming skills will typically need a bachelor's degree—or at least an associate's degree—to land an entry-level position at a strong company. Programmers study mathematics, information science, and computer science at universities. For those who want to advance and get more involved in software development, a master's degree can help. Top colleges for computer science include the Massachusetts Institute of Technology, Stanford University, and Cornell University, but nearly every college in the United States offers at least some form of computer-based degree path.

Nothing provides a better education than hands-on training, and most colleges offer internship programs that give students the chance to work in a real-life business environment while earning course credit.

For those who want to advance in a programming career, higher education is often the best option. Many colleges across the country offer degree programs to master coding skills.

Thousands of corporations take on interns to assist in technology-related tasks, including Apple, General Electric, Hewlett-Packard, Verizon, IBM, Boeing, Microsoft, Comcast, and many more. Interns may participate in searching for solutions to problems that only code can crack. They also may play a role in developing software to carry out vital tasks. In addition, interns make job connections with other professionals who may be the link to other employment opportunities. Most people develop their careers through networking, and the internship experience strengthens a résumé, especially for someone just entering the industry.

Glossary

Boolean A variable having only one of two possible values, often "true" or "false."

Cascading Style Sheets (CSS) A tool mainly used to define the look and feel of websites; CSS code often determines design and layout.

class A form of code that defines operations and describes data fields.

conditional A programming statement that assesses the value (commonly "true" or "false") of a certain condition and does different things depending on that assessment.

database A structured set of data in a computer.

debugging The process of finding and fixing errors in software and hardware.

format The way data is saved or presented.

GIF Short for "graphics interchange format," this media format is used for short, repeating animations.

Hypertext Markup Language (HTML) The language most commonly used to create websites, HTML tells a browser how to display graphics, text, and other elements.

macro Short for macroinstruction, a macro is a small program that automates certain tasks.

MP3 A technology format that compresses sounds or music to small files that can be digitally stored and transmitted.

open-source Describing a computer program that provides free access to code for the general public to use and modify.

operating system The software that supports a computer's basic functions.

pixels The very small light-emitting components that make up the displays of computer monitors.

platform An environment in which software operates.

relative path A way of finding or calling a file based on its directory location.

software Programs used to operate computers.

span Used in HTML code, span defines part of a document so it is identifiable.

variable An element that can be changed and evaluated as a program runs.

For More Information

Canada Learning Code
129 Spadina Avenue
Toronto, ON M5V 2L3
Canada
(647) 715-4555
Website: http://canadalearningcode.ca
Facebook: @canadalearningcode
Twitter and Instagram: @learningcode
This organization has a mission to provide digital skills
    to all Canadians—especially women, girls, people
    with disabilities, indigenous youth, and newcomers to
    the field.

Canadian Advanced Technology Alliance (CATA)
207 Bank St. Suite 416
Ottawa, ON K2P 2N2
Canada
(613) 236-6550
Website: http://www.cata.ca
Twitter: @CATAAlliance
The largest high-tech association in Canada, CATA is a
    comprehensive resource for the latest high-tech news
    in Canada.

Canada's Association of Information
    Technology Professionals
1375 Southdown Road

Unit 16 - Suite 802
Mississauga, ON L5J 2Z1
Canada
(905) 602-1370
Website: http://www.cips.ca
Facebook: @CIPS.ca
Twitter: @CIPS
This association offers networking opportunities, certification, and accreditation for various fields in computer science.

Code.org
1501 4th Avenue
Seattle, WA 98101
Website: http://code.org
Facebook: @Code.org
Instagram and Twitter: @codeorg
This nonprofit organization focuses on expanding access to computer science in schools and increasing participation of women and underrepresented minorities.

CompTIA/Association of Information Technology Professionals (AITP)
3500 Lacey Road, Suite 100
Downers Grove, IL 60515
(866) 835-8020
Website: https://www.aitp.org
Facebook: @comptiaaitp
Twitter: @comptia
This worldwide society of professionals in information technology offers career training, scholarships, news, and social networking opportunities.

National Association of Programmers
PO Box 529
Prairieville, LA 70769
Website: http://www.napusa.org
This professional trade organization is dedicated
    to providing information and resources to help
    programmers, developers, consultants, and students in
    the computer industry.

For Further Reading

Bedell, Jane. *So, You Want to Be a Coder? The Ultimate Guide to a Career in Programming, Video Game Creation, Robotics, and More*. New York, NY: Aladdin, 2016.

Ford, Melissa. *Writing Interactive Fiction with Twine*. Indianapolis, IN: Que Publishing, 2016.

Guthals, Stephen Foster, and Lindsey Handley. *Modding Minecraft: Build Your Own Minecraft Mods!* Hoboken, NJ: Wiley, 2015.

Harris, Patricia. *Understanding Coding Through Debugging*. New York, NY: PowerKids Press, 2017.

Lyons, Heather, Elizabeth Tweedale, and Alex Westgate. *Kids Get Coding: A World of Programming*. Minneapolis, MN: Lerner Publications, 2016.

Mayer, Brian. *Create Interactive Stories in Twine*. New York, NY: Rosen Publishing, 2019.

Wainewright, Max. *How to Code: A Step-By-Step Guide to Computer Coding*. Asheville, NC: Sterling Children's Books, 2016

Wood, Kevin. *Get Coding with Logic*. New York, NY: Windmill Books, 2018.

Ziter, Rachel. *Coding from Scratch*. North Mankato, MN: Capstone Press, 2018.

Bibliography

Converse, Grace. "Hypertext and Destiny: This Twine Could Be Your Life." Rhizome, August 20, 2014. http://rhizome .org/editorial/2014/aug/20/twine-could-be-your-life.

Ellison, Cara. "Anna Anthropy and the Twine Revolution." *Guardian*, April 10, 2013. https://www.theguardian.com /technology/gamesblog/2013/apr/10/anna-anthropy -twine-revolution.

Friedhoff, Jane. "Untangling Twine: A Platform Study." Digital Games Research Association. Retrieved April 22, 2019. http://www.digra.org/wp-content/uploads/digital -library/paper_67.compressed.pdf.

Garbade, Michael. "Top 3 Most Popular Programming Languages in 2018 (and Their Annual Salaries)." Hackernoon.com, August 30, 2018. https://hackernoon .com/top-3-most-popular-programming-languages-in -2018-and-their-annual-salaries-51b4a7354e06.

Hammond, Adam. "A Total Beginner's Guide to Twine 2.1." AdamHammond.com. Retrieved April 8, 2019. http:// www.adamhammond.com/twineguide.

Hudson, Laura. "Twine, the Video Game Technology for All." *New York Times*, November 19, 2014. https://www .nytimes.com/2014/11/23/magazine/twine-the-video -game-technology-for-all.html.

Occupational Outlook Handbook. "Computer Programmers." Bureau of Labor Statistics, April 12, 2019. https://www.bls.gov/ooh/computer-and-information -technology/computer-programmers.htm.

Parrish, Allison. "A Quick Twine (2.2+) Tutorial."
    Computational Approaches to Narrative. Retrieved April
    8, 2019. http://catn.decontextualize.com/twine.
Peery, Bridget, Cody Mello-Klein, and Rachel Grozanick.
    "How to Use Twine to Build an Interactive Story with
    Data." Ruggles Media, March 7, 2017. http://www
    .northeastern.edu/rugglesmedia/2017/03/07/how-to
    -use-twine-to-build-an-interactive-story-with-data.

Index

I

J

K

L

M

N

O

P

Q

R

S

About the Author

Don Rauf is the author of numerous nonfiction books, including *Getting to Know Java*; *Getting Paid to Manage Social Media*; *Lost America: Vanished Civilizations, Abandoned Towns, and Roadside Attractions*; and *Killer Lipstick and Other Spy Gadgets*. He lives in Seattle with his wife, Monique, and son, Leo.

Photo Credits

Cover Mr.Whiskey/Shutterstock.com; cover, p. 1 (code) © iStockphoto.com/scanrail; p. 5 Mr.Cheangchai Noojuntuk/Shutterstock.com; p. 7 aslysun/Shutterstock.com; p. 8 iinspiration/Shutterstock.com; p. 47 Monkey Business Images/Shutterstock.com; p. 50 rafapress/Shutterstock.com; p. 51 South_agency/E+/Getty Images; interior pages border design © iStockphoto.com/Akrain.

Design: Matt Cauli; Editor: Siyavush Saidian; Photo researcher: Sherri Jackson